Hi, kids! It's me, Eleanor! My friends and I are going to have lots of fun exploring Color World and Shape Land. Do you want to come along with us? I hope so!

See these stars? Each time you learn something new, you get one of these star stickers to put on your train ticket. When you finish a whole section, you'll get a big train car sticker to put on your train track Certificate of Completion at the end of the book.

See this picture of me? When you see it on the page, it means I'm there to help you. Just look for **Eleanor's Tips**.

Ready for our adventure? Here we go! Toot, toot!

There are so many places to go in Color World.
Help us find our way.
Draw a line from each  **to its matching color in the picture.**

What is your favorite color?
Circle the ticket.

Let's play Toss the Ball!
Draw a line between each  **and its matching color** .

Can you say the name of each color?

Great work! Put your star sticker on your train ticket. Now jump ahead to the next level.

Eleanor's Tips

Yellow is the color of the ☀.

Casey's favorite color is yellow.
Help us find all the yellow ⬭'s.
Put an X on each one.

Can you name two more things that are yellow?

Eleanor's Tips

Blue is the color of my eyes.

Eleanor's favorite color is blue.
**Help us buy all the blue 's.
Circle each one.**

Can you name two more things that are blue?

Eleanor's Tips

When you mix **blue** ✳, and **yellow** 🌼, you make **green** 🌿. Green 🌿 is the color of a 🐸.

Kisha's favorite color is green. **Help us win the green** 🐸 **for Kisha. Draw a line from the** ⭕ **to each of the green** 🎳**'s.**

Look around. Can you name two more things that are green?

Pierre's favorite color is red.
Put an X on the red 's.

You did it! Now place a star sticker on the train ticket and jump ahead to the next level.

Red 🔴, yellow 🟡, and blue 🔵 are called **primary** colors. When you put them together they make different colors.

Look! We each won a prize. **Help us take our prizes home. Circle the ones that match the colors of our tickets.**

Look! We each won a  for our fancy cakes.
Can you tell which ones we baked?
Circle the cakes that match the color of our ribbons.
Then color in the last cake in each row any color
you like!

Wow! You get a star sticker for your train ticket!
Now jump ahead to see what you have learned.

Come with us over the rainbow! We want to find the pot of gold.

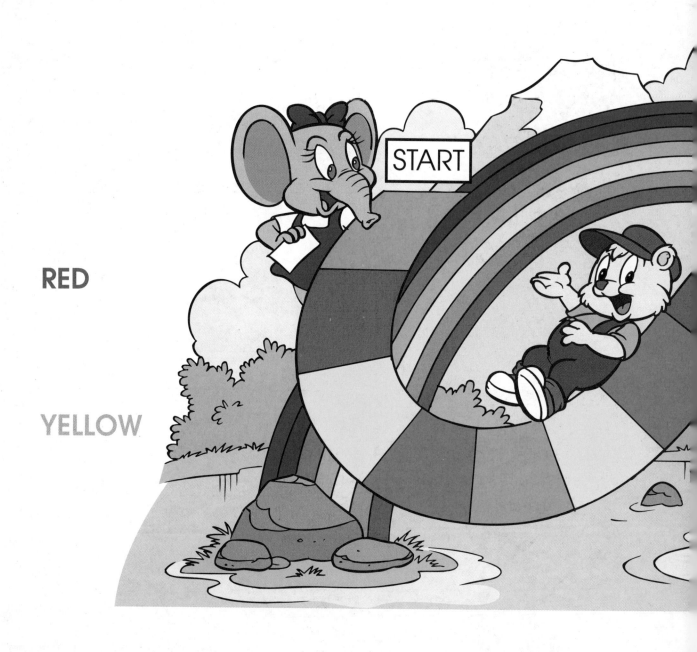

RED

YELLOW

Start at the first color square. Put your finger on it. Can you name it? Then move your finger to the next color square and name it, too. Keep going until you've won the pot of gold!

GREEN

BLUE

FINISH

Can you draw a line from each of the color names to a matching color square?

Super! Place a big train car sticker on your Certificate of Completion and jump ahead.

Review 11

Eleanor's Tips

These shapes are made from **straight** lines.

Rectangle Diamond Square Triangle

Toot! Toot! Here we are in Shape Land. Help us find our way around.

Draw a line from each ■ ◆ ■ △ **to something in the picture that has the same shape.**

Even the clouds here have special shapes.
Draw a line from each to the 👟
with the same shape.

Wonderful work! Place your star sticker on
your train ticket and jump ahead to the next level.

Eleanor's Tips

A ● is **round** and has no corners. The ☀ is shaped like a circle.

Let's play. How many ●'s can you find in the sandbox? **Put an X on each one.**

Look around. Can you think of two more things that are shaped like circles?

Eleanor's Tips

A ■ has **four sides**.
A ▨ is shaped like
a **square**.

Kisha wants to climb
the jungle gym.
**Put an X on all the ■ 's
you see.**

**Look around. Can you find two more things
that are shaped like squares?**

Eleanor's Tips

A ▲ has **3 sides**. 🍕 is shaped like a **triangle**.

Casey wants to go sailing. Before he goes, he must find the ▲'s.
Put an X on each triangle. How many did you find?

Look around you. Can you find one more thing that is shaped like a triangle?

Oops! I lost my kite.

Help me find it. Trace all the shapes. What else do you see in Shape Land? Color in the picture!

Eleanor's Tips

A ▲ is still a ▼ even when it's **upside down**.

Kisha is great at drawing shapes! **Look at her picture in the sand. Then trace the same shapes in my sandbox.**

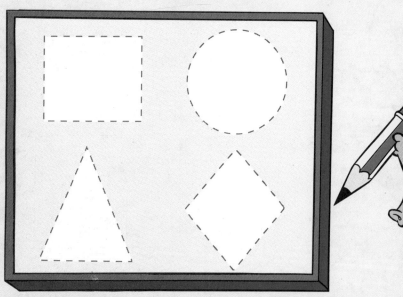

Now you can color in your sand picture.

What's a picnic without good things to eat?

A  is a ▢. Color mine in.
Pierre's □ is also a ▢. Color it in.
Casey's 🍕 is a △. Color it in.
Kisha's ⬤ is a ◯. Color it in.

You're doing great! Take a star sticker and put it on your train ticket. Jump ahead!

Let's have a picnic in the park!
Help us make a quilt to sit on.
Read the key and decorate the quilt.

KEY

○ = red   △ = yellow   ▭ = green

▢ = orange   ◇ = blue   any other shape = purple

Excellent! Place a big train car sticker on your Certificate of Completion and jump ahead.

Review **21**

Toot! Toot! Here we are at Kisha's Diner. Kisha just baked a 🎂.

Can you draw a line from each ⬤ to the same-sized layer on the cake?

Point to the smallest ⬤.
Then point to the biggest.

Let's go to Kisha's Diner for cookies.
Where does each belong?
Draw a line from each to the right .

You're doing great! Place a star sticker on your train ticket and jump ahead to the next level.

Sizes **23**

Kisha needs your help!
Put the  on the table from shortest to tallest.
Draw a line from each to each friend.
Casey gets the shortest stack.

Who has the most pancakes?

You're just in time for a cold drink!
Put an X on the empty  .
Circle the that has a little water.
Underline the that is full.

Now use a crayon to fill the empty glass almost to the top!

More and **less** are words that compare how much.

Casey likes fish. I like peanuts. Put an X on the 🥏 that has more food on it.

Now add a treat you like to the 🥏 that has less.

Those  sure look good.
Casey wants the plate with the most pie.
I want the one with the least.
Draw a line from each of us to the right .

Great job! Put a star sticker on your train ticket and jump ahead to the next level.

See these empty 's?
Use your crayons to fill them up in order from full to empty.

What kind of drinks did you give us?

I can bake a cake just like Kisha's. Do you want to help?

Use crayons to decorate the layers of your special cake from biggest to smallest.

All aboard! It's almost time to leave. Let's get all the train cars ready.

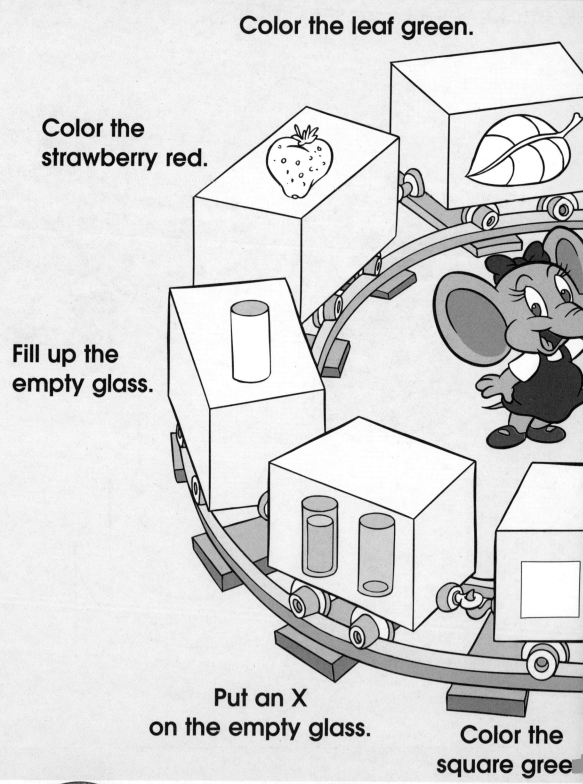

Color the leaf green.

Color the strawberry red.

Fill up the empty glass.

Put an X on the empty glass.

Color the square gree[n]

Follow the directions next to each car.

Color the orange orange.

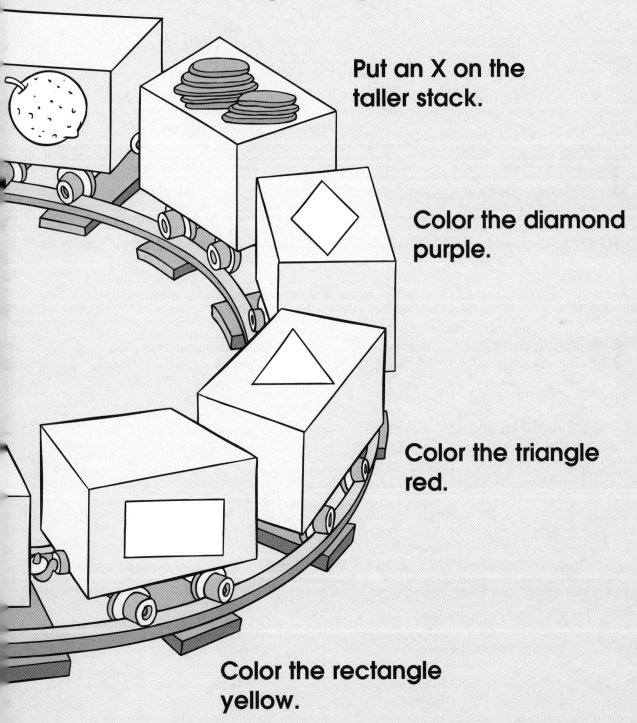

Put an X on the taller stack.

Color the diamond purple.

Color the triangle red.

Color the rectangle yellow.

Great job! Place your big train car sticker on your Certificate of Completion. You did it!

Review **31**

Answer Key

PAGE 2   Lines connect yellow, blue, red, green tickets to matching colors in picture

PAGE 3   Lines connect colored balls to matching color bowls

PAGE 4   Draw X's on eight yellow balls

PAGE 5   Circle the two blue balloons

PAGE 6   Draw lines from green ring to five green pins

PAGE 7   Draw X's on five red apples

PAGE 8   Circle the red teddy bear; blue whale; green frog; yellow lion

PAGE 9   Circle the purple cake; yellow cake; pink cake; orange cake

PAGE 10–11   Name each color; draw lines from each name to the matching colored squares

PAGE 12   Draw lines from diamond to kites and Eleanor; from rectangle to sandbox and Kisha; from square to jungle gym and Casey; from triangle to sailboat and Pierre

PAGE 13   Draw lines from triangle to Pierre's shoe; from circle to Casey's shoe; from square to Eleanor's shoe; from diamond to Kisha's shoe

PAGE 14   Draw X's on 11 circles

PAGE 15   Draw X's on twelve squares

PAGE 16   Draw X's on three triangles

PAGE 17   Trace all the shapes; color in the picture

PAGE 18   Trace the four shapes; color in the sand picture

PAGE 19   Color two square sandwiches; a triangular slice of pizza; a circular orange

PAGE 20–21   Color in shapes corresponding to key

PAGE 22   Draw lines connecting cake layers to matching layers on three-layer cake

PAGE 23   Draw lines between same-sized cookies

PAGE 24   Draw lines from Casey to the middle stack; from Pierre to left stack; from Eleanor to right stack; Eleanor has the most pancakes

PAGE 25   Draw an X on Kisha's glass; circle Pierre's glass; underline Casey's glass

PAGE 26   Draw an X on Casey's plate; draw your own treat on Eleanor's plate.

PAGE 27   Draw a line from Casey to plate with four slices; draw a line from Eleanor to plate with one slice

PAGE 28   Color glasses in this order: full, half full, empty

PAGE 29   Decorate three-layer cake, beginning with largest layer ending with smallest

PAGE 30–31   Follow instructions next to each car